ISOLDE

ISOLDE. FROM "THE STUDIO"

THE
LATER WORK
OF
AUBREY
BEARDSLEY

DOVER PUBLICATIONS, INC., NEW YORK

This Dover edition, first published in 1967, is an unabridged republication of the revised 1930 edition of the work originally published by John Lane, The Bodley Head. The present edition differs in the following respects:

All plates which were better printed in editions prior to that of 1930 have been reproduced here from those earlier editions.

Two of the four plates printed in color in earlier editions (there was no color in the 1930) are reproduced here in color, in addition to their black-and-white reproductions in the 1930 numerical sequence. The other two plates, Nos. 75 and 76 of the present volume, were originally printed in green ink.

The frontispiece and title-page frame of the original editions now appear in their proper numerical sequence as Plates 1 and 2.

Library of Congress Catalog Card Number: 67-21706

MANUFACTURED IN THE UNITED STATES OF AMERICA

DOVER PUBLICATIONS, INC.
180 VARICK STREET
NEW YORK, N.Y. 10014

LIST OF PLATES

LIST OF PLATES

* Also in color between Plates 20 and 21.   † Also in color as the frontispiece.

LIST OF PLATES

LIST OF PLATES

LIST OF PLATES

PUBLISHER'S NOTE

MY warmest thanks are due to Mr. Frederick H. Evans for his assistance in tracing several drawings, the existence of which was unknown to me; also to the possessors of originals, whose name I give beneath each plate, by whose courtesy I have been enabled to reproduce many hitherto unpublished specimens of Beardsley's work.

There has been considerable rearrangement of the plates. Many that originally appeared in the "Early Work" are now transferred to this volume, and conversely, in order to preserve a proper chronological sequence.

PLATES

From a private portrait study by Frederick H. Evans.

Aubrey Beardsley.

Plate I

Plate 2

Plate 3

DESIGN FOR FRONTISPIECE OF
"PLAYS," BY JOHN DAVIDSON

Plate 4

DESIGN FOR TITLE-PAGE OF
"PLAYS," BY JOHN DAVIDSON

THE YELLOW BOOK

AN ILLVSTRATED QVARTERLY.

BOOKS

PRICE
FIVE SHILLINGS

ELKIN MATHEWS
AND JOHN LANE,
THE BODLEY HEAD
VIGO ST. LONDON.

APRIL 15ᵗ
MDCCC XCIV.

Plate 5

DESIGN FOR COVER OF "THE
YELLOW BOOK" PROSPECTUS

Plate 6

Plate 7

DESIGN FOR REVERSE COVER
OF "THE YELLOW BOOK"

Plate 8

TITLE-PAGE ORNAMENT FOR "THE
YELLOW BOOK," VOLUME I ❦ ❦

Plate 9

L'ÉDUCATION SENTIMENTALE.
FROM "THE YELLOW BOOK,"
VOLUME I

Plate 10

NIGHT PIECE. FROM "THE
YELLOW BOOK," VOLUME I

PORTRAIT OF MRS. PATRICK CAMPBELL.
FROM "THE YELLOW BOOK," VOLUME I

Plate 11

Plate 12

Plate 13

COVER DESIGN FOR "THE YELLOW BOOK," VOLUME II

Plate 14

TITLE-PAGE ORNAMENT FOR "THE
YELLOW BOOK," VOLUME II ❦ ❦

Plate 15

COMEDY-BALLET OF MARIONETTES, I
FROM "THE YELLOW BOOK," VOLUME II

Plate 16

COMEDY-BALLET OF MARIONETTES, II
FROM "THE YELLOW BOOK," VOLUME II

Plate 17

COMEDY-BALLET OF MARIONETTES, III
FROM " THE YELLOW BOOK," VOLUME II

Plate 18

GARÇONS DE CAFÉ. FROM "THE YELLOW BOOK," VOLUME II ℣

Plate 19

THE SLIPPERS OF CINDERELLA. FROM
"THE YELLOW BOOK," VOLUME II

Plate 20

PORTRAIT OF MADAME RÉJANE. FROM
"THE YELLOW BOOK," VOLUME II

MADAME RÉJANE

Plate 21

COVER DESIGN FOR "THE YELLOW
BOOK," VOLUME III ❧ ❧ ❧

Plate 22

TITLE-PAGE DESIGN. FROM "THE
YELLOW BOOK," VOLUME III

ANDREAS. MANTEGNA.
PAINTER.
AND.
ENGRAVER. OF PADVA.
1L.91 — 1506.

Plate 23

PORTRAIT OF MANTEGNA (BY PHILIP
BROUGHTON). FROM "THE YELLOW
BOOK," VOLUME III

Plate 24

PORTRAIT OF HIMSELF. FROM "THE YELLOW BOOK," VOLUME III ꙮ ꙮ

Plate 25

LADY GOLD'S ESCORT. FROM "THE
YELLOW BOOK," VOLUME III ❦ ❦

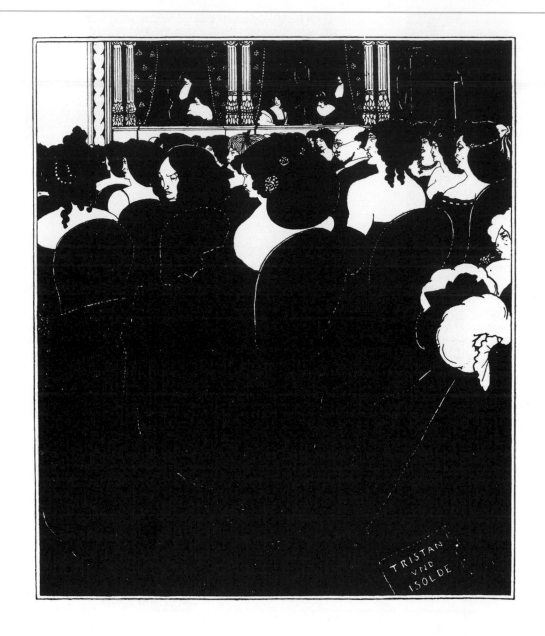

Plate 26

THE WAGNERITES. FROM "THE
YELLOW BOOK," VOLUME III ❦

Plate 27

LA DAME AUX CAMÉLIAS. FROM
"THE YELLOW BOOK," VOLUME III

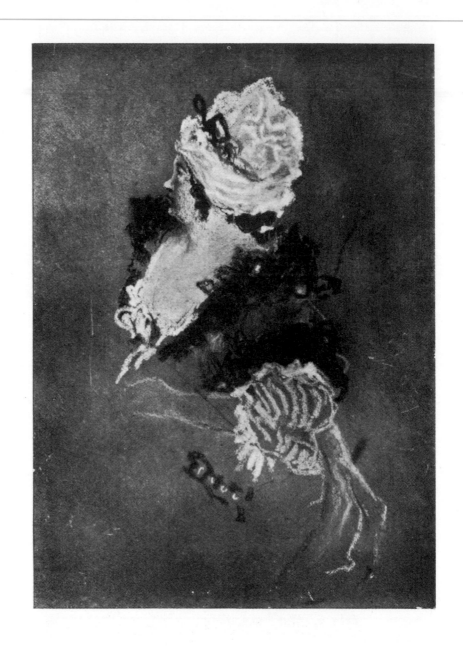

Plate 28

"FROM A PASTEL" (BY ALBERT FOSCHTER). FROM "THE YELLOW BOOK," VOLUME III ❧ ❧ ❧

Plate 29

COVER DESIGN FOR "THE
YELLOW BOOK," VOLUME IV

Plate 30

DESIGN FOR TITLE-PAGE. FROM
"THE YELLOW BOOK," VOLUME IV

THE MYSTERIOUS ROSE GARDEN.
FROM "THE YELLOW BOOK,"
VOLUME IV

Plate 31

THE REPENTANCE
OF MRS . . . .

Plate 32

THE REPENTANCE OF MRS. . . .
FROM "THE YELLOW BOOK,"
VOLUME IV

Plate 33

PORTRAIT OF MISS WINIFRED
EMERY. FROM "THE YELLOW
BOOK," VOLUME IV

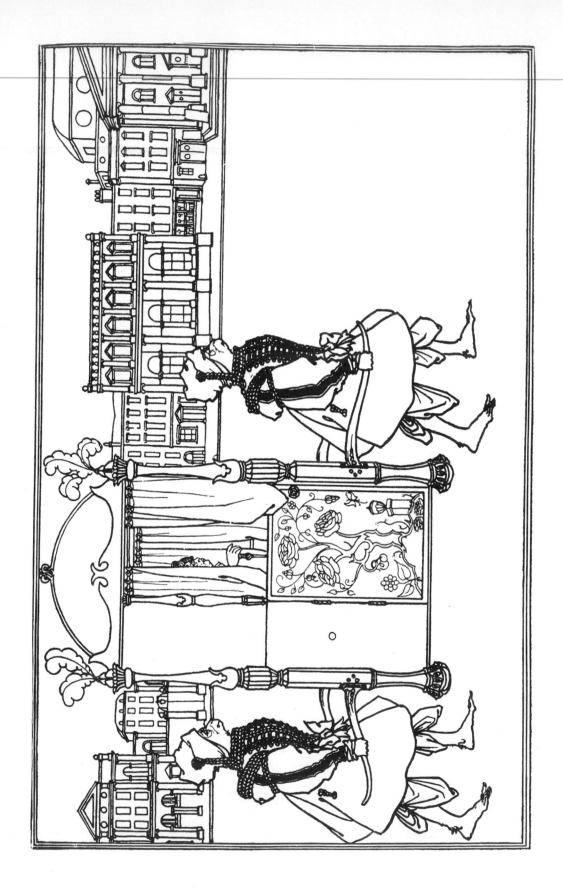

Plate 34

FRONTISPIECE FOR "JUVENAL." FROM
"THE YELLOW BOOK," VOLUME IV

Plate 35

FROM THE FRONTISPIECE FOR
THE SIXTH SATIRE OF JUVENAL
(UNPUBLISHED)

Plate 36

DESIGN FOR "YELLOW BOOK"
COVER (NOT USED)

Plate 37   A POSTER FOR "THE YELLOW BOOK"

Plate 38

MADAME RÉJANE

Plate 39

MADAME RÉJANE.   REPRODUCED
BY PERMISSION OF MR. R. B. ROSS

Plate 40

MADAME RÉJANE.   REPRO-
DUCED BY PERMISSION OF
MR. FREDERICK H. EVANS
This plate also appears in color be-
tween Plates 20 and 21.

Plate 41

A POSTER

Plate 42

A POSTER DESIGN. FIRST REPRODUCED
IN "THE POSTER," OCTOBER" 1898

VENUS.

FRONTISPIECE. FOR "VENUS
AND TANNHÄUSER"

Plate 43

THE STORY OF VENUS AND TANNHÄUSER, IN WHICH IS SET FORTH AN EXACT ACCOUNT OF THE MANNER OF STATE HELD BY MADAM VENUS, GODDESS AND MERETRIX, UNDER THE FAMOUS HÖRSELBERG, AND CONTAINING THE ADVENTURES OF TANNHÄUSER IN THAT PLACE, HIS REPENTANCE, HIS JOURNEYING TO ROME, AND RETURN TO THE LOVING MOUNTAIN. By AUBREY BEARDSLEY.

FRONTISPIECE AND TITLE-PAGE FOR "VENUS AND TANNHÄUSER"

Plate 44

THE RETURN OF TANNHÄUSER TO
VENUSBERG. REPRODUCED BY
PERMISSION OF MR. J. M. DENT

Plate 45

Plate 46

DESIGN FOR TITLE-PAGE
("VENUS")

Plate 47

DESIGN FOR COVER OF "THE CAM-
BRIDGE A.B.C." BY PERMISSION OF
THE REV. W. AUSTEN LEIGH

AVBREY
BEARDSLEY

Plate 48

DESIGN FOR A GOLF CARD
BY PERMISSION OF MR. R. HIPPESLEY COX

Plate 49

A POSTER DESIGN. BY PERMISSION
OF MR. WILLIAM HEINEMANN

Plate 50

AUTUMN. FROM A DESIGN FOR A
CALENDAR. BY PERMISSION OF
MR. WILLIAM HEINEMANN ❧ ❧

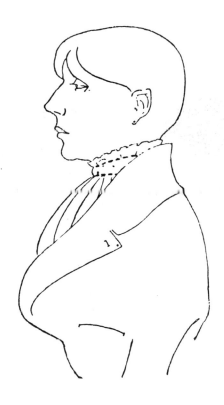

Plate 51

OUTLINE PORTRAIT OF HIMSELF.
FROM "POSTERS IN MINIATURE"

Plate 52

A CHILD AT ITS MOTHER'S BED.
FROM "THE SKETCH." BY PER-
MISSION OF MR. MAX BEERBOHM

Plate 53   THE SCARLET PASTORALE

Plate 54

DESIGN FOR AN INVITATION
CARD   ❦   ❦   ❦

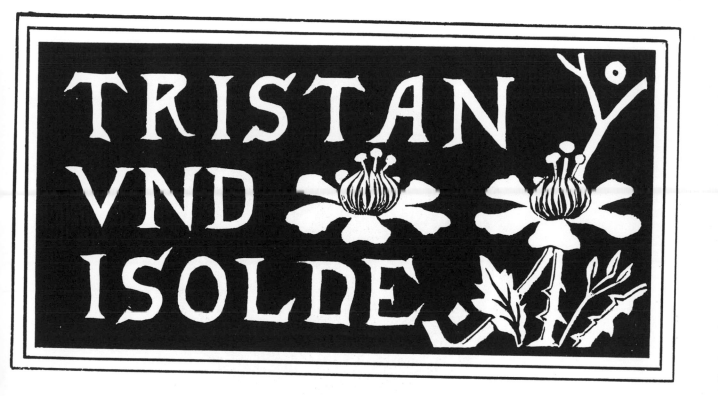

Plate 55

DESIGN FROM THE COVER OF AUBREY
BEARDSLEY'S COPY OF "TRISTAN
UND ISOLDE." BY PERMISSION OF
MR. F. H. EVANS

Plate 56

ISOLDE

ISOLDE. FROM "THE STUDIO."
BY PERMISSION OF MR. CHARLES
HOLME 🦋 🦋 🦋 🦋
*This plate also appears in color as the fron-
tispiece.*

Plate 57

Plate 58

DESIGN FOR A BOOK
COVER ℰ ℰ

Plate 59   A CATALOGUE COVER

Chopin. Ballade III. Op 47.

CHOPIN, BALLADE III. OP. 47. FROM "THE STUDIO." BY PERMISSION OF MR. CHARLES HOLME

Plate 60

Plate 61   A NOCTURNE OF "CHOPIN"

Plate 62

DESIGN FOR FRONTISPIECE OF "EARL
LAVENDER." BY PERMISSION OF
MESSRS. WARD AND DOWNEY

Plate 63   MESSALINA

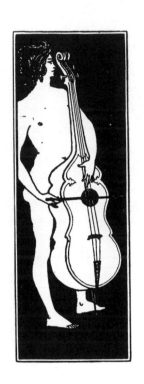

Plate 64   TITLE-PAGE ORNAMENT

Plate 65

PORTRAIT OF MISS LETTY LIND

Plate 66

ATALANTA

COVER DESIGN (SIDE). FROM
BALZAC'S "LA COMÉDIE
HUMAINE" ❧ ❧ ❧

Plate 67

Plate 68

COVER DESIGN (BACK). FROM
BALZAC'S "LA COMÉDIE
HUMAINE" ❧ ❧ ❧

Plate 69

DESIGN FOR FRONTISPIECE TO "AN
EVIL MOTHERHOOD." BY PERMIS-
SION OF MR. ELKIN MATHEWS

Plate 70

BLACK COFFEE

Plate 71

DESIGN. FROM THE TITLE-PAGE
OF "THE PARADE"

Plate 72

DESIGN FOR COVER OF
WHARTON'S "SAPPHO"

Plate 73

Plate 74

AVBREY BEARDSLEY.

DESIGN FOR END-PAPER OF "PIERROT"

Plate 75

Plate 76

AVBREY BEARDSLEY

DESIGN FOR END-PAPER OF "PIERROT"

Plate 77

DESIGN FOR REVERSE COVER
OF "PIERROT"   ❧   ❧

LYSISTRATA.

Plate 78

LYSISTRATA
THIS AND THE FOLLOWING SEVEN DESIGNS
APPEARED IN A PRIVATELY PRINTED EDITION
OF THE "LYSISTRATA" OF ARISTOPHANES

Plate 79   LAMPITO

Plate 80

LYSISTRATA HARANGUING THE
ATHENIAN WOMEN

Plate 81

A DESIGN

AVBREY
BEARÒSLEY

Plate 82

AN ATHENIAN WOMAN

Plate 83   MYRRHINA

Plate 84

THE HERALD

Plate 85   A DESIGN

THE DREAM 🐛 🐛 🐛
THIS AND THE FOLLOWING EIGHT DESIGNS
ARE REPRODUCED FROM "THE RAPE OF THE
LOCK," PUBLISHED BY JOHN LANE 🐛

Plate 86

Plate 87

THE BILLET-DOUX

Plate 88

THE TOILET

Plate 89

THE BARON'S PRAYER

Plate 90

THE BARGE

Plate 91

THE RAPE OF THE LOCK

Plate 92

THE CAVE OF SPLEEN

Plate 93

THE BATTLE OF THE BEAUX
AND THE BELLES

Plate 94

THE NEW STAR

Plate 95

COVER DESIGN (REDUCED). FROM
THE ORIGINAL EDITION OF "THE
RAPE OF THE LOCK" ❧ ❧

Plate 96

COVER DESIGN. FROM THE BIJOU
EDITION OF "THE RAPE OF THE
LOCK," PUBLISHED BY JOHN LANE

Plate 97   A CATALOGUE COVER

AVBREY BEARDSLEY

Plate 98

DESIGN FOR THE PROSPECTUS
OF "THE SAVOY"

Plate 99

ANOTHER DESIGN FOR THE PROSPECTUS
OF "THE SAVOY"

Plate 100

INITIAL. FROM THE PROSPECTUS
OF "THE SAVOY"   ❦   ❦

Plate 101

SIEGFRIED

THE SAVOY

AUBREY BEARDSLEY. 1896.

Plate 102

COVER DESIGN. FROM "THE SAVOY
NO. 1, PUBLISHED BY JOHN LANE

THE SAVOY

AUBREY
BEARDSLEY.
1896.

TITLE-PAGE. FROM "THE SAVOY,"
NOS. 1 AND 2

Plate 104

THE THREE MUSICIANS.   FROM
"THE SAVOY," NO. 1   ❧   ❧

Plate 105

Plate 106

THE THREE MUSICIANS. ANOTHER
DESIGN, WHICH WAS NOT USED IN
"THE SAVOY"

Plate 107

TAILPIECE TO "THE THREE MUSICIANS" ❦ ❦ ❦
THIS AND THE FOLLOWING THIRTY-THREE DESIGNS ARE REPRODUCED FROM "THE SAVOY," PUBLISHED BY JOHN LANE ❦

Plate 108

ON DIEPPE BEACH
(THE BATHERS)

MOSKA

Plate 109

THE MOSKA

THE ABBÉ

THIS AND THE FOUR DESIGNS WHICH FOLLOW
APPEARED IN "THE SAVOY," NO. 1, AS ILLUS-
TRATIONS TO "UNDER THE HILL," A ROMANTIC
NOVEL, BY AUBREY BEARDSLEY

Plate 110

Plate 111

THE TOILET OF HELEN

Plate 112

THE FRUIT-BEARERS

Plate 113   A CHRISTMAS CARD

Plate 114   COVER DESIGN. FROM "THE SAVOY," NO.

AB

Plate 115

A FOOTNOTE

Plate 116

SAINT ROSE OF LIMA

Plate 117

THE THIRD TABLEAU OF
"DAS RHEINGOLD"

Plate 118   COVER DESIGN.   FROM "THE SAVOY," NO. 3

THE
SAVOY

Plate 119

PUCK. FROM "THE SAVOY,"
PUBLISHED BY JOHN LANE

AUBREY BEARDSLEY.

THE COIFFING
THIS AND THE FOLLOWING DESIGN APPEARED
IN "THE SAVOY," NO. 3, ILLUSTRATING "THE
BALLAD OF A BARBER," BY AUBREY BEARDSLEY

Plate 120

Plate 121   CUL-DE-LAMPE

Plate 122

COVER DESIGN. FROM "THE SAVOY," NO. 4

GIULIO FLORIANI.

Plate 123   COVER DESIGN. FROM "THE SAVOY," NO. 5

Plate 124

THE WOMAN IN WHITE

Plate 125

THE FOURTH TABLEAU OF
"DAS RHEINGOLD"

THE DEATH OF PIERROT
"AS THE DAWN BROKE, PIERROT FELL INTO HIS LAST SLEEP. THEN UPON TIPTOE, SILENTLY UP THE STAIR, NOISELESSLY INTO THE ROOM, CAME THE COMEDIANS, ARLECCHINO, PANTALEONE, IL DOTTORE, AND COLUMBINA, WHO WITH MUCH LOVE CARRIED AWAY UPON THEIR SHOULDERS THE WHITE-FROCKED CLOWN OF BERGAMO; WHITHER, WE KNOW NOT"

AUBREY BEARDSLEY

Plate 126

Plate 127   COVER DESIGN. FROM "THE SAVOY," NO. 7

AVE ATQVE VALE

Plate 128

AVE ATQUE VALE: CATULLUS,
CARMEN CI

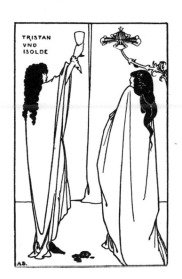

Plate 129

TRISTAN UND ISOLDE

Plate 130   COVER DESIGN. FROM "THE SAVOY," NO. 8

Plate 131

A RÉPÉTITION OF "TRISTAN
UND ISOLDE"

Plate 132

DON JUAN, SGANARELLE,
AND THE BEGGAR. FROM
MOLIÈRE'S "DON JUAN"

MRS PINCHWIFE

Plate 133

MRS. PINCHWIFE

THE
COMEDY
OF
THE
RHINEGOLD

Plate 134

Plate 135

FLOSSHILDE. TO ILLUSTRATE
"DAS RHEINGOLD"

ERDA

Plate 136

ERDA. TO ILLUSTRATE
"DAS RHEINGOLD"

Plate 137

ALBERICH. TO ILLUSTRATE
"DAS RHEINGOLD"

Plate 138

FELIX   MENDELSSOHN
BARTHOLDY   🎵   🎵

Plate 139

CARL MARIA VON WEBER

Plate 140

COUNT VALMONT. FROM "LES
LIAISONS DANGEREUSES"

Plate 141

ET IN ARCADIA EGO

PENCIL SKETCH OF A CHILD. BY
PERMISSION OF MR. FREDERICK
H. EVANS ❧ ❧ ❧ ❧

Plate 142

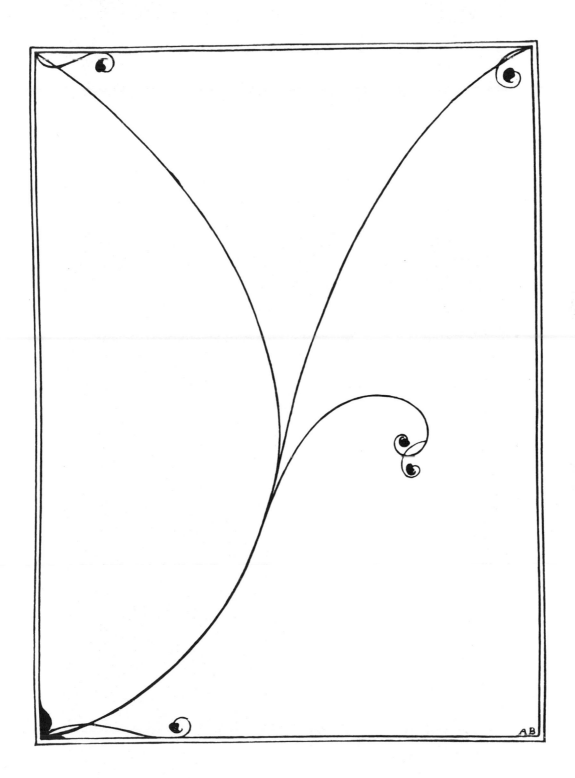

Plate 143

COVER DESIGN. FROM "VERSES,"
BY ERNEST DOWSON

Plate 144

FRONTISPIECE
THIS AND THE FOLLOWING THREE DESIGNS
APPEAR IN THE POEMS OF ERNEST DOWSON,
PUBLISHED BY JOHN LANE

Plate 145

HEADPIECE

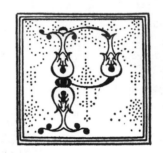

Plate 146   INITIAL

Plate 147

CUL-DE-LAMPE

THE PIERROT OF THE MINVTE.

Plate 148

COVER DESIGN. FROM "THE PIERROT OF THE MINVTE," PUBLISHED BY JOHN LANE

Plate 149

COVER DESIGN. FROM "THE
SOUVENIRS OF LEONARD"

BOUTEZ EN AVANT ·

COVER DESIGN. FROM "THE
LIFE AND TIMES OF MADAME
DU BARRY"

Plate 150

Plate 151

FRONTISPIECE. FROM "A
BOOK OF BARGAINS"

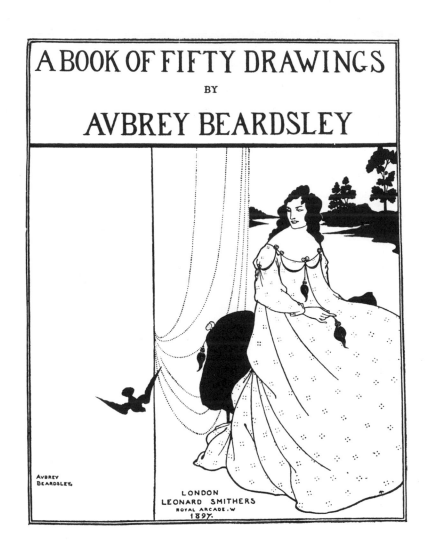

Plate 152

COVER DESIGN. FROM "A
BOOK OF FIFTY DRAWINGS"

Plate 153

SILHOUETTE OF AUBREY
BEARDSLEY

Plate 154

AUBREY BEARDSLEY'S
BOOK-PLATE ❦ ❦

ALI BABA

Plate 155

COVER DESIGN FOR "THE FORTY THIEVES"

Plate 156

ALI BABA IN THE WOOD

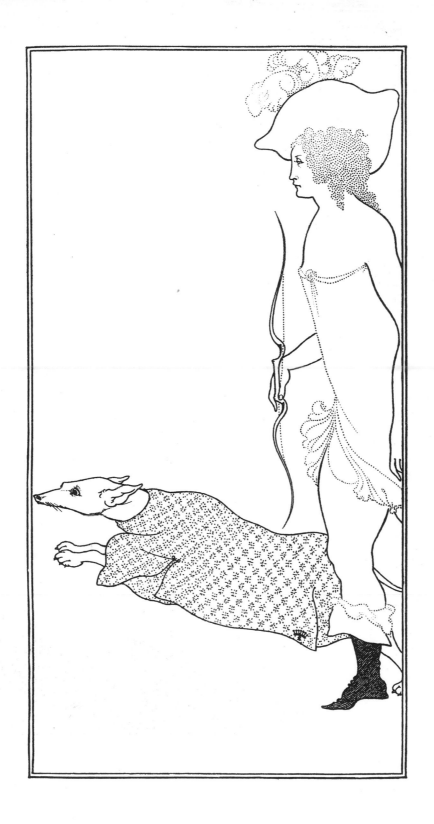

Plate 157

ATALANTA

MESSALINA.

Plate 158

MESSALINA RETURNING FROM
THE BATH ❦ ❦ ❦

Plate 159

COVER DESIGN. FROM
"THE HOUSES OF SIN"

Plate 160

LA DAME AUX CAMÉLIAS.
REPRODUCED BY PERMIS-
SION OF MR. R. B. ROSS

EX LIBRIS
OLIVE
CVSTANCE

Plate 161

BOOK-PLATE.   BY   PERMISSION
OF MISS OLIVE CUSTANCE (LADY
ALFRED DOUGLAS) ❧   ❧   ❧

MADEMOISELLE DE MAUPIN

Aubrey Beardsley pinx

MADEMOISELLE DE MAUPIN
THIS DESIGN, WITH THE FIVE THAT
FOLLOW, APPEARED AS ILLUSTRATIONS
TO THÉOPHILE GAUTIER'S ROMANCE
"MADEMOISELLE DE MAUPIN" 𝄢

Plate 162

Plate 163   D'ALBERT

Plate 164

D'ALBERT IN SEARCH
OF IDEALS ❧ ❧

Plate 165

THE LADY AT THE
DRESSING-TABLE

Plate 166

THE LADY WITH THE ROSE

Plate 167   THE LADY WITH THE MONKEY

VOLPONE

Plate 168

COVER DESIGN. FROM
"VOLPONE," PUBLISHED
BY JOHN LANE ❦ ❦

VOLPONE

FRONTISPIECE
THIS AND THE FOLLOWING FIVE DESIGNS
ARE FROM "VOLPONE," BY BEN JONSON.
PUBLISHED BY JOHN LANE

Plate 169

Plate 170

INITIAL

Plate 171

INITIAL

Plate 172

INITIAL

Plate 173

INITIAL

Plate 174   INITIAL

Dover Books on Art

THE FOUR BOOKS OF ARCHITECTURE, Andrea Palladio.
A compendium of the art of Andrea Palladio, one of the most
celebrated architects of the Renaissance, including 250 mag-
nificently-engraved plates showing edifices either of Palladio's
design or reconstructed (in these drawings) by him from clas-
sical ruins and contemporary accounts. 257 plates. xxiv + 119pp.
9½ x 12¾.   T1308 Clothbound $10.00

150 MASTERPIECES OF DRAWING, A. Toney. Selected by a
gifted artist and teacher, these are some of the finest drawings
produced by Western artists from the early 15th to the end of
the 18th centuries. Excellent reproductions of drawings by Rem-
brandt, Bruegel, Raphael, Watteau, and other familiar masters,
as well as works by lesser known but brilliant artists. 150 plates.
xviii + 150pp. 5⅜ x 11¼.   T1032 Paperbound $2.00

MORE DRAWINGS BY HEINRICH KLEY. Another collection
of the graphic, vivid sketches of Heinrich Kley, one of the most
diabolically talented cartoonists of our century. The sketches
take in every aspect of human life: nothing is too sacred for him
to ridicule, no one too eminent for him to satirize. 158 drawings
you will not easily forget. iv + 104pp. 7⅜ x 10¾.
                                             T41 Paperbound $1.85

*THE TRIUMPH OF MAXIMILIAN I, 137 Woodcuts by Hans
Burgkmair and Others.* This is one of the world's great art
monuments, a series of magnificent woodcuts executed by the
most important artists in the German realms as part of an
elaborate plan by Maximilian I, ruler of the Holy Roman Empire,
to commemorate his own name, dynasty, and achievements. 137
plates. New translation of descriptive text, notes, and bibliography prepared by Stanley Appelbaum. Special section of 10pp.
containing a reduced version of the entire Triumph. x + 169pp.
11⅛ x 9¼.   T1207 Paperbound $3.00

PAINTING IN ISLAM, Sir Thomas W. Arnold. This scholarly
study puts Islamic painting in its social and religious context
and examines its relation to Islamic civilization in general. 65
full-page plates illustrate the text and give outstanding examples
of Islamic art. 4 appendices. Index of mss. referred to. General
Index. xxiv + 159pp. 6⅝ x 9¼.   T1310 Paperbound $2.50

*THE MATERIALS AND TECHNIQUES OF MEDIEVAL
PAINTING, D. V. Thompson.* An invaluable study of carriers
and grounds, binding media, pigments, metals used in painting,
al fresco and al secco techniques, burnishing, etc. used by the
medieval masters. Preface by Bernard Berenson. 239pp. 5⅜ x 8.
                                             T327 Paperbound $1.85

*THE HISTORY AND TECHNIQUE OF LETTERING, A.
Nesbitt.* A thorough history of lettering from the ancient Egyp-
tians to the present, and a 65-page course in lettering for artists.
Every major development in lettering history is illustrated by a
complete aphabet. Fully analyzes such masters as Caslon, Koch,
Garamont, Jenson, and many more. 89 alphabets, 165 other specimens. 317pp. 7½ x 10½.   T427 Paperbound $2.00

LANDSCAPE GARDENING IN JAPAN, Josiah Conder. A detailed picture of Japanese gardening techniques and ideas, the artistic principles incorporated in the Japanese garden, and the religious and ethical concepts at the heart of those principles. Preface. 92 illustrations, plus all 40 full-page plates from the Supplement. Index. xv + 299pp. 8⅜ x 11¼.

T1216 Paperbound $2.75

DESIGN AND FIGURE CARVING, E. J. Tangerman. "Anyone who can peel a potato can carve," states the author, and in this unusual book he shows you how, covering every stage in detail from very simple exercises working up to museum-quality pieces. Terrific aid for hobbyists, arts and crafts counselors, teachers, those who wish to make reproductions for the commercial market. Appendix: How to Enlarge a Design. Brief bibliography. Index. 1298 figures. x + 289pp. 5⅜ x 8½.

T1209 Paperbound $1.85

THE STANDARD BOOK OF QUILT MAKING AND COLLECTING, M. Ickis. Even if you are a beginner, you will soon find yourself quilting like an expert, by following these clearly drawn patterns, photographs, and step-by-step instructions. Learn how to plan the quilt, to select the pattern to harmonize with the design and color of the room, to choose materials. Over 40 full-size patterns. Index. 483 illustrations. One color plate. xi + 276pp. 6¾ x 9½.

T582 Paperbound $2.00

LOST EXAMPLES OF COLONIAL ARCHITECTURE, J. M. Howells. This book offers a unique guided tour through America's architectural past, all of which is either no longer in existence or so changed that its original beauty has been destroyed. More than 275 clear photos of old churches, dwelling houses, public buildings, business structures, etc. 245 plates, containing 281 photos and 9 drawings, floorplans, etc. New Index. xvii + 248pp. 7⅞ x 10¾.

T1143 Paperbound $2.75

A HISTORY OF COSTUME, Carl Köhler. The most reliable and authentic account of the development of dress from ancient times through the 19th century. Based on actual pieces of clothing that have survived, using paintings, statues and other reproductions only where originals no longer exist. Hundreds of illustrations, including detailed patterns for many articles. Highly useful for theatre and movie directors, fashion designers, illustrators, teachers. Edited and augmented by Emma von Sichart. Translated by Alexander K. Dallas. 594 illustrations. 464pp. 5⅛ x 7⅛.

T1030 Paperbound $2.75

Dover publishes books on commercial art, art history, crafts, design, art classics; also books on music, literature, science, mathematics, puzzles and entertainments, chess, engineering, biology, philosophy, psychology, languages, history, and other fields. For free circulars write to Dept. DA, Dover Publications, Inc., 180 Varick St., New York, N.Y. 10014.